WRITTEN HERE

The Community of Writers Poetry Review 2018

Editor-in-Chief
　Masha Lisak

Editorial board
　Judy Brackett Crowe
　Christine H. Cummings
　Nancy Kangas
　Diane Martin
　Joan Baranow
　Ted Lardner
　Jack Martin
　Kate O'Neill

Book design and production
　Cody G. Gates & Maureen Forys, Happenstance Type-O-Rama

Cover photograph
　Christopher Upham

Cover design
　Cody G. Gates, Happenstance Type-O-Rama

Copyright ©2019 The Community of Writers at Squaw Valley

ISBN-13: 978-0-9888953-5-5

All rights reserved. No part of this journal may be reproduced or republished without written consent from the publisher, except by reviewers who may quote brief excerpts in connection with a review in a newspaper, magazine, or electronic publication; nor may any part of this journal be reproduced, stored in a retrieval system, or transmitted in any form without written consent of the publisher. However, contributors maintain ownership rights of their individual poems and as such retain all rights to publish and republish their work.

WRITTEN HERE 2018

OUR DEEPEST THANKS
TO THE STAFF POETS, 2018

Kazim Ali
Mónica de la Torre
Robert Hass
Sharon Olds
Evie Shockley
Dean Young

CONTENTS

Catherine Staples	WHAT THE POEM WANTS, DAY FOUR	1
Kazim Ali	PULSE	3
Elizabeth Biller Chapman	I CALL IT DEEP POOL	5
Armen Davoudian	KAYAK	6
Sharon Olds	CON TCILF	8
Jay Brecker	FLUIDITY	9
Jacqueline Hughes Simon	NAMING RIGHTS FOR FIRES	10
Jabari Jawan Allen	CENTO	11
Dan Alter	POEM WITH DISHES & DEAD SEA	12
Ethan Andrews	ROUTINES	14
Joan Baranow	RED	15
Sherah Bloor	UNTITLED GATHERING #4	16
Jeremy Cantor	ENVY	18
James Ciano	FIRST	19
Jolie Elizabeth Clark	WHEN GOD WOULDN'T STAY OFF HER TEETH,	21
Judy Brackett Crowe	THIS BOY	22
Rosa De Anda	CLOCK	23
Michael Anna de Armas	DIAMONDS IN THE SPINE	24
Julie Sevilla Drake	TO NOT BE FROM THERE IS TO NOT BE	25
Danny Duffy	ODE TO HEMORRHOID	27
Jay A. Fernandez	BLOOD	29
Kelsey Gutierrez	UNLEARNING FLIGHT	31

Jessica Guzman	DEAD HAND	33
donia salem harhoor	thoth's bill	34
Hannah Hirsh	CONFESSIONAL AS PRIMAL SCREAM	35
Brionne Janae	AUBADE	37
Nancy Kangas	THE END	38
Genevieve Kaplan	AT THE FOUNTAIN THERE IS MUSIC	40
Ariana-Sophia Kartsonis	SQUAWBERRY MOON	41
Victoria Kornick	IVIG	42
Ted Lardner	SOMETIMES WHEN SOMETHING SADDENS ME I GROW MEAN	44
Jessica Lee	MY MOTHER IS LEARNING IN HER AUTHENTIC RELATIONSHIPS COURSE	45
Kateema Lee	WE CARRY	46
Rob Lipton	GRACE	47
Masha Lisak	TO BRODSKY	49
Emily Luan	池上	50
Christine H. Cummings	CONFESSION	51
Laurie Macfee	CENTO OF BOOKS I'VE FOUND	52
Diane K. Martin	THE LAST TIME	54
Veronica Martin	GLOVING	55
Daria-Ann Martineau	SUDDEN AND NOT SO	56
Nick Maurer	WESTERN MOTEL	58
Florencia Milito	TOTEM ANIMAL	59
Kate O'Neill	INCOMING STORM	60
Pamela Paek	COLON: AERIAL VIEW TWO PEOPLE, BACKS TURNED	61

Yamini Pathak	DHARMA	62
Sarah Peace	IF EVER	63
Emily Pérez	JEFFREY PINE	64
Michael A. Reyes	TODDLER	66
Corinna Rosendahl	NO HUNGRY	69
Kalen Rowe	MY BIG STUPID BIGOT STATE	71
Brett Shaw	WHEN YOU ARE AWAY ALL MY MEMORIES ARE TACTILE	76
Michael Sinck	[IF YOU READ THIS BEAR DON'T BE SCARED WE'RE BACK WALKING THE DEERPATH BEHIND YOUR DAD'S HOUSE]	78
Kathleen L. Taylor	SELVING	79
Jay Aquinas Thompson	THEY HAVE TAKEN ME FROM THE WORLD	80
Eden Werring	THE TWO EDENS	83
Emily Wolahan	ALL TALES ENORMOUSLY UNKNOT MEMORY	85
Marcene Gandolfo	BEES IN WINTER	88
Jack Martin	CROSSING THE RIVER	89
Bob Hass	CONFESSIONAL POETRY	92
Evie Shockley	in) visibility	95
Charles Halsted	THE YEAR THE SOX WON THE PENNANT	96
Tamam Kahn	THE WELL AND BABA FARID	98
Mónica de la Torre	DIVAGAR	99
Jesse Nathan	POEM	101
The Poets		102

WHAT THE POEM WANTS, DAY FOUR

The poem wants its own birds, not these pre-dawn chorusers.
It wants the southern slope of the meadow and hummingbirds,
two hummingbirds starting up from the sage,
that whirring you hear before you see them, full
opposite of the pandemonium crows are raising now
which sounds like ode to a parking lot.
The crows are amusing themselves, poem is unimpressed.
Poem wants a tent of bedclothes and more sleep.
It's tired of being chased. All these pillows
and sheets to bar the morning light. It wants toast,
it has wanted toast all week and would like
to let you know you're a poor listener for a poet.
It can't quite forgive you for forgetting your swimsuit,
it wanted lakewater in its hair more
than anything, head under and quiet and leave me alone.
It knows you ought to have just done
what you did at a Glassilaun last summer,
only the mountains and a few German hikers watching.
The poem has had it with intention, it wants sleep.
It wants to walk, walk off the path into that marsh
where blueberries grow and find the bears, well,
one bear, and if you insist on staying on the sand path,
it wants lupine in its buttonholes, it wants summer
before summer is over. A single bear downhill
through scree, the dank smell of danger
and ice and falling. The poem is homesick
for the wood thrush, the way she sings and whole tracts
of forest rise unfolding, doubling. Oh, and the poem

wants to sleep with your husband, it's been up late, thinking.
It wants a tent of bedclothes lifting like a sail in wind,
It wants irons, a flying jibe, the smallest hummingbird—
pollen on its forehead as it flits through your open window
thinking penstemon, bee balm, bottlebrush, beardstongue.

PULSE

To the sharp report in the dark the season comes home

Long tongue sound between hand and arm between mouth
    and flesh

Hold this moment river still what if it was my life

To return after years to the same province of danger

An old town you know like the handle the bump stock
    the trigger

I want to return to the boat that bore me from the far shore
    decades ago

What I lived in those languages I forgot the places I left
    that I want to return to

Were we seen were we spoken were all the wolves baying

Met at the edge of the bright darkness of rain

Time cannot fulfill its promise to splinter return or slow

Vow this wheel this we will this weal we even wean

We in the world would wolve a low vow foaled

Worn low at the hip to be a solid soldier who sold his
    soiled soul

For the chance to be the first to aim first to fire to fly

In the cross hairs I am heir to no oar to hold I am on both
    sides of the gun

Toll as sound or cost one that never ends and the other
    never returns

Any embrace is the first error in meanings slope

Wrought by thought that one could reach another touch
    his shape

Known in two genders like Orlando whose tongue newly
    woke

To pronounce any word for god or man means to enter
    violence's fold

No oath sworn to save no salvation no salve no valor no
    ovation no nation

Elizabeth Biller Chapman

I CALL IT DEEP POOL

The last painting you made for me,
its blues so saturate, the paper nearly sodden,
I imagine it still damp to the touch.
No time for a formal border, you
sketched the interrupted black lines of one
whose breathing came, often, staggered then.

What do I call the place I'm in,
its weather? the weather of it,
the cold wet fog or heavy mist?
In Suffolk, maybe, "sea-fret."
           I do love a spondee.

I'm still finding Post-its you'd hide
when I was out of the room:
"Against all odds, I find I still love you."
Who else in the world would print
on a bright blue square, "Tout est possible, Fifi,"

and paste it to my notebook?
People said, "He was old." Why, yes he was.

I hear that some familiar birds of summer
are disappearing now, their cries few and faint
that once were numerous among the meadow hay.
           Corncrake. Grex grex. Nightjar.

Armen Davoudian

KAYAK

O mock
    hammock
unyoked
    unquayed
shark-skegged
    silt-sprayed
sea-sled
    limber
limb of
    limping
lumber
    yawn-mawed
gewgaw
    womb of
wood tomb
    rocking
like mad
    mid lake
among
    amok
mean peaks
    that pour
in your
    wound slot
a sad
    salt lot
in sunlight
    in water
in withershins
    weather

all bird
      no feather
I whimper
      you wamble
you yaw
      I stumble
I weary
      you worry
brother
      I'm sorry

Sharon Olds

CON   TCILF

By day, stretching my greenish-grey
arms up into the blue altitude.

                       ,maerd ym ni nerdlihc gnimrah ,thgin yB
                          ,meht gniticxe-revo yldliw ,meht gnilkcit
                                        .em ekil lliw yeht os

The swallow floats . . .
cuts the air —
veers.

                                tew lacitrev fo ffilc a gnibmilC
                 . . . seimene ym fo ecneserp eht ni spets etinarg

Underwater this year, the lake's stripes —
citrine, turquoise, green, silver —
blur into each other.

                      — tius a ni nam a ,spets eht fo pot eht tA
                           evol gnikam fi sa mih gnihcuot
                                .xes ylno si ti tub ,mih ot

Waking, despairing, disgusted.

                                   gniyas nerdlihc ehT
                           .rehtom rou eb ot <u>mih</u> tnaw ew

But you already have a mother,

                                  .rehtom ruoy ton <u>m'I</u>

No longer dreaming of being harmed.

                            .remrah eht gnieb fo gnimaerD

No longer dreaming of my own grown children.
Sonando con los ninos de Mexico.

Jay Brecker

FLUIDITY

Three
boys —
hatless in
still air late
in the day, walk
barefoot look down
to place their feet, pay
no attention to slip-slides
of eave-dwelling birds above
— pick a path upward. The sun
should be in their eyes. They wear
wetsuits. Why? For protection from
insects rising out of yellow mule's ear
ticking up along the route? Are they lost? Lost
like us among strangers and old acquaintances,
like three boys among lodgepole pines where it feels
safe to catch our breath at altitude? Are there hordes of
us holding our breath? Selfishly? Has oxygen in the hot
dry late day air oxidized? To rust our lungs? To remind us
of old gills? To search for wetsuits before neoprene's price
floats higher as demand is strong and land unremitting? Unlike
plains, deserts, mountains, forgotten cities, farms, suburbia —
a rumor to begin with — could we survive? The sea rise is
a growth situation. Recognize those boys walking in
wetsuits on the mountain as a deity. A new Trinity.
We suit up with fear, head for cliffs, to beaches,
any inlet to leap, plunge and mass beneath
the water, never to see what surrounds
us gone, burnt, choked-off beyond
salvation. We pray to be baptized.
We pray let us be sanctified
in fluid greed.

Jacqueline Hughes Simon

NAMING RIGHTS FOR FIRES

:: We almost lived here once,
    a long time ago ::

:: *Datura* dripping night scent ::

:: Open-skinned visions
    of bare branches & wires ::

:: Spring quince   flowering
    plum   cherry   pear   trees with the fruit bred out of them ::

:: Remember the grey-cold green
    of western waves ::

:: Palms snapped from the top ::

:: We built a shelter of our skin   there was nothing to
    prevent us from burning ::

:: What went up in the blaze
    nests lined with willow cotton   deer hair   vole fur

    feathers & fine grass ::

Jabari Jawan Allen

CENTO

Surely that act was not divided

        in the branches of the laurel tree

where you have thrown me, scraped me with your kiss:

        moonlight streamed inside as if it had been

            clinging to my head & hands.

    Even without faith

(the death we said we both outgrew),

        I have returned here a thousand times

            until the wound widened

in a dead white mist—

        What was the harm?

        A luna moth in a chambered cage

under the night somewhere?

        We accepted this: a land without light excited us—

Dan Alter

POEM WITH DISHES & DEAD SEA

Sun going   she showed him
how to wash the whole

sinkful with half the water sun
gone   So much

was new   Desert residue
went leaking from the helter-skelter

Jerusalem-stone houses   In the dark
he was swollen with her body's

words   pillow trickle hum

Voices runneled from windows
piled up on all sides   She held

a hand toward him in kindness
while her eyes continued to the humid

valley   onion fields   vines
raising fruit up trellises in rows

full of distance   Her friends   also older
took their last sparkling sentences

away to sleep   From kitchens of triple
exiled Kurdish Jews   air dusted

with crushed seeds & pepper
passed their courtyard on its way

down barrens to the lowest place
on earth

        By morning
on the table a torn open

sheet of the feather-thin blue

paper they had once used to fly
what they felt around the world

Ethan Andrews

ROUTINES

I am not of this world

Well perhaps that's overstating it

Some mornings I never leave the shower

Just stay in there drawing steam faces until I can't
see my hands— those are the good days

Others I wake up and my heart has become a second
Appendix— disconnected it goes on beating

Like a dog chasing its tail or a man revisiting a grave
I keep circling the spot like a flannel tornado

Or a detective with no leads or a closet-trapped simile
I am not of this world

Others— wake up! My heart has become a second
Mouth and has something very urgent to tell you:
Don't go it alone

There are bears and crumbling precipices
And who will you share your sandwich with?

RED

Paper hearts cut with safety scissors.
Jack knife. Chipped nail polish.
Crescent of kiss on the cup.

Brash snow plant
in a field of needles. The plaid shirt
of the wildflower expert.

Alizarin crimson dabbed on the palette.
She squints to see the skin's flush.
Drapery. Genital petals.

Strips snagged from the breast
stained for the diagnosis.
The pathologist's bitten lip.

A winter dawn.
The last flash before the earth
turns away.

Sherah Bloor

UNTITLED GATHERING #4

Though he's assured *God, give me
what is good for me* is safe to pray
Andrew hears it as a threat. As
Shirin pouring out the sweet sahlep
whispers *flowers here are plastic.*
And when the waiter hands over
a damp peony she turns pink-
faced to the wall. On its other side
a chef, a Chishti Dervish, quarters heads
of lettuce. Tells the family Maryam's
disease was disappointment. Above
town in a boardroom, it is be
decided. Child soldiers are shipped
from Sierra Leone to Iraq. *It is not
good. It is not good,* Mamadu shakes
his head. *Just a little sweetness,*
her granny spoons more honey
into Lily's milky tea. Sara sits up
in her very own bed to say *I want
to go home.* Samiya too is ten-feet up
in a corner of perception as if
behind one of the long black wings
where from that angle, the dancers.
Wants to call out *I'm floating*
but her mum opens the dishwasher
to feel its good hot vapour and
greets Salih, who, having returned
from the walk around the plot, wants
to speak. To say down near the mill
where kids stand in the water wheels
he saw a sheep part-paralysed

with brain worm, had no rifle or knife,
with only his hands, he dug a hole
into the ground, carried the body,
felt its breath against his arm and
all the while screaming, buried it still alive.

Jeremy Cantor

ENVY

I envy the fanatic because he has no doubts
the skeptic because he has no certainty

the dolphin because she moves in three dimensions

the mathematician because she moves in two, but dreams
    in many

the earthworm because it only needs be concerned with
    one dimension
the geometric point because it has none but feels no lack

the lion because everyone fears him
the butterfly because no one does

the hawk because he dreams of nothing he cannot do

the ant because she is never lonely

I envy the honeybee because she always knows her way home

FIRST

Earlier, I was so moved
by how the cream looked
when I poured it into the coffee,
that I had to stop and watch it,
and for a minute, held up the line
behind me, and wanted to yell
to each person *Hey have YOU seen this?!*
Such flushedness is what I thought,
like I imagine the feeling of walking
to the edge of a roof and not walking
off, the wanting-to-live-again
suddenly rushing back into the body,
the gravel on the roof, the rust
on the link fence. It's in the way
the cream expands like a galaxy
or the body overcome by one
of those breezes that makes you
start to cry or how when I think
about my mother dying
all I can do is begin to run,
or dance, but not dancing
in a beautiful way, something very ugly,
something so instinctual
that if someone saw they might
think *holy fuck* and then pull
out their phone and take a video
and I'd look like a string puppet
played with by a toddler
in a basement as his mother sits
upstairs smoking at the kitchen
counter and thinking about the many
ways her life could've been different

and wasn't and the video would
become mildly popular on the internet
and might, in bed late at night, make
someone in a different state who has given
up on their dream of being a dancer
think wow, this guy's good, this guy's
got it. How helpless I am to do anything
but imagine how one day all the people
I love won't be people anymore but will
be abnormally large pine cones, or winds
through oaks and the light that falls
through them off-white like cosmic dust
or the dog swimming in the river,
the one with a stick in its mouth
or a can or a rock, the dog that leaves
the rock at my feet and even when
I throw it again into the river
the dog doesn't chase after,
she waits for me to dive in first.

Jolie Elizabeth Clark

WHEN GOD WOULDN'T STAY OFF HER TEETH,

she knew it was time to go back home,
get back down on her knees and stay there awhile,
she had not grown up with a particularly wrathful god
but when her teeth kept falling out with the pop pop of
summer corn shucked into a metal bucket
her mother said, "you better start praying,
you never know what certain men will do to get you back,
climb the sky in a fury, crack the trellis of your bones on
    the pavement."

She thought of the way certain things are only
quantified by their absence: her mother, beautiful,
in the way that the buildings in the old films are beautiful,
trembling as the earth shakes. Her father, ashes sprinkled
beneath the bed of poppies in the backyard,
their colors violent and unnatural.

At night, her childhood bed bucked beneath her and
    she slept
with her hands wrapped tight across her mouth, holding
    it all in,
together, her teeth loosening in her mouth, determined not
to say, for once, what needed saying. Downstairs her
    mother sang,
sang. And did not bleed. This had to be enough, didn't it?

Judy Brackett Crowe

THIS BOY

They say the heartache/heartbreak/agony
of defeat is the price we pay,
the sacrifice we make,
the contract we sign
so someone else
can slap the high fives,
wear the laurel,
bathe in euphoria,

but this boy signed no contract—
this boy knows only that he lost,
that he has failed
once again,
and he will leave that field
and fight off tears and self-loathing
once again.

Not knowing if it will be her last escape,
she scrubs the kitchen sink, scours the toilet,
tosses moldy bread and rotting fruit,
makes the bed with fresh sheets,
and, a wry smile to herself,
reckons it's all the same as hoping
she'll be wearing pretty, clean underwear
when the fall or the crash or her body's last
protest happens,

and if she finds herself back here again,
god-willingly or not,
she will sit in the red chair by the window,
drink a cup of tea,
think about that boy, gone now,
think about supper.

Rosa De Anda

CLOCK

Dressed in ashes of our past you are the sadness in my eyes.
Between reason and tradition I hear your soundless contempt
more blinding than the sun. Fog in my throat hold on to my
song. My hips adorned by ocean waves clapping furious
flamenco storms. Mordant copper glitter sands I will not dance.
I will not stomp upon caged children's dreams from any shore.
Children. Discarded garbage. I look at you and drown in smoke—
parents mourn your loss re-cutting scars and abundant smiles.
Twenty-four thousand obsidian eyes regale an absent God. Red
soaked cockpits flying feathers; gleaming blades and mariachi
songs were not enough. Detonate.

Forget. All. I let a seven-headed angel scratch my dreams;
I sucked her breasts milked her truth arresting beauty and
protruded sex. She asked me for my life, I said, "Not just yet."
Winds of seduction spread wilting flowers but not their scent.
Propagate. Propagate your word. Stand! I birthed death when
I was born cut my teeth on sinner's breath, ensconced putrid
lies within my folds and multiplied, multiplied like endless
Goddesses reborn.

Scream. Unclench. Divine sacred sacrifice you love the
sweetness of our blood. Pulverize all pussy hats stitch their
See-through lips castigate all Witches burn their spells and
books intercede all prayers shut down every school fill their
hungry minds with empty wishes and... dried tits. Hydrate.
Dance.

Michael Anna de Armas

DIAMONDS IN THE SPINE

When Willie Merwin translated *diamante* in Dante's Purgatorio as *adamant*, the dreams started. Person after person, some familiar but most not, with diamonds in their spines. Exactly like studs, round, brilliant cut, right on or adjacent to vertebra, just one sparkling pageant of will power, one jet pack of indissolvable determination ringing directly the central nervous system, each like the night skies couldn't trust us anymore or once stars outnumbered a certain infinity, they needed to directly deposit starlight so rays of medieval mystery give us a mineralogical brightness where we could never see but our friends might maybe discover on a brave shirtless afternoon.

Julie Sevilla Drake

TO NOT BE FROM THERE IS TO NOT BE

In the old life,
I fished, subsistence
dipnet deep in the tide,
days spent bobbing like a seal,
chest-high at the confluence
of glacial river and ocean,
the only forward view
a horizon of sea stopped by snow-topped smoking
    volcanoes, indomitable possibilities. In the old
life, I went to empty spaces
to get empty. Curious,
once, I asked my sister's husband
what do you think about when you stand in this water,
    waiting for fish to rattle your net?
His answer,
nothing.
He is Inupiaq from way far north, so when he says nothing
    in his hollow voice, I hear all
of nothing—
tundra and enormous expanses where rolling land meets
    sky greets treeless mind.
Nothing is
isn't:
a place
to land, get lost,
to rest or to roam,
a space glacier-cold, a gift luxurious as oily fish. Slipping
    away. Nothing ordinary, nothing
grand. Language, a village, a river knee-deep with
    uncounted silvers. Enough. A blessing, cursed.

In the old days,
nothing was stolen
from his people. All people.
Nothing given in return.
In my old life, he and I shared our two families' salmon
    limits, and we thought nothing of it.
(Against the law, but fuck 'em all.)

Danny Duffy

ODE TO HEMORRHOID

Gatekeeper—
Your soft mole nose
Popped out of its burrow,
Weary of insects, worms,
And other creeps
I may have let slide.

When you swelled
I had to kill you.
And besides, I wanted
To be made anew.
I wanted to love
These cells
Just a little more,

But the pain that came
After your departure
Made that impossible.
You made it
So that no one
Could use your burrow
Without you.

Yesterday,
In the shower,
I thought I may have
Met your kin
Looking for a drink
Of water.

As wonderful
As it would be
To have an excuse
For everything,
It seems unfair
For nature

To reclaim the body
I never actually
Made mine.

Jay A. Fernandez

BLOOD

At nine or ten you'd huddle there, you
        And your brother, dropped in the lap of an
Overwhelmed aunt, soft superior untested
        Cherubs touring Hell's day care. Thrown
In with coarse cousins rattling in the sad
        Vacuum of the Seventies, wardens of an old
Victorian that taunted the phony peace
        Of the suburbs' futile scrawl. *They are your*

Blood, you're told, *your people*. The claim
        Bleaches and haunts. You'd hold out your
Hand in nervous offering to snarling (smiling)
        Beasts, weigh invitations to break unproven
Pledges in a West Philly *Lord of the Flies*—
        No authority figure, no moral fencing,
Marine father permanently reassigned to
        The Polish secretary on Brunswick Ave. The

Treehouse with working electricity they'd
        Wired themselves. Motorcycles in the listing
Barn stabled like bitter stallions. Life material-
        Izing as a knife blade through the calf, a bullet
Hole in the bannister, a jar of peanut butter
        Topless in the sun. Fun shaped into diversions
Feral treacherous and hard. They hugged
        The bored July days then shook them down

As if they owed money, like juice men who'd
        Happily break arms for free. It was hotwired blue
Mustangs and the graceless joy of nights spilled
        Drunk as a puddle under trucks in gravel lots,

Bar lights and moonshine cutting their unlaced
        Boots and unplugged minds. It was pipe joints
And flanges, gear boxes and manifolds, a stolen
        Stereo receiver. It was Louis L'Amour and Billy

Joel's *52nd Street* and George Carlin's "Seven
        Words." It was the lovely lonely defilements of a
Midnight round of Truth or Dare, girls stripped
        Of secrets like torn-away skirts, your ambivalence
Knotted by desire. These beautiful, rough-edged
        Boys were America's truest-born sons. And look
At them now: loyal, reckless, a pack of hungry
        Dogs scouring the neighborhood, scent of blood

Rimming the nostrils, a nation's angry pride branded
        On their skin. And you: still a witness tallying scores,
Swaddled in condescension, envy in every stranded
        Boast, spinning tribal stories as if they were yours.

Kelsey Gutierrez

UNLEARNING FLIGHT

By the light of an infomercial shilling a better mousetrap,
my sternum turns to shrapnel and erupts from my chest.
I must be dead, I must be dying, this must be the end.
The full-body terror of my first panic attack detonates my logic
like a landmine, spews viscera all over the as-seen-on-TV.

In the back of an ambulance I can't remember calling,
my ragged breath fogs the oxygen mask. I fumble jellied
fingertips from collarbone to xiphoid, study my salt-slicked
skin for punctures, tendon-torn confetti to explain
the incandescence slicing through my baffled nerves.

The first responder fills a syringe. I mean to mouth no, don't,
but my teeth lock into my lip. *Please, you don't understand,*
I want to shout, *you can't make me like her.*
Fingers flick the barrel, push ten uninvited milligrams—in
seconds, my heart is velvet, my lungs are oil-slicked tires
on a highway after the first real drops of rain. I stop sipping air
and breathe, finally breathe, but god, at what cost?

The soft light of a memory catches on something sharp
in my gut, breaks a little: I am eight again, riding alongside
as she writhes on a gurney, mewling for those opioid wings.
My mother, the trick candle, could never seem to put herself out—
threw back benzo blues and hot pink prescription pills
until they stained her, a kaleidoscope of self-medicated sunrises
and sunsets caught from the back window of an ambulance.

Neurons reassemble, latex-laden fingers squeeze my shoulder
as if checking the ripeness of fruit at the market. I am solid at last.

I try and fail to forget the rapid onset of injectable calm
and the way my body flourished under its touch. I am furious
at a gloved pair of hands for allowing me to soar past panic
on alkaloid feathers I'll tell myself I do not want to keep.

DEAD HAND
after W.S. Merwin

Like temptations
to touch still

ponds, frogs, a nest
settled in

a low branch. It
browns, fingers

like tongues
of basilisks

curl, hang
from the blanket

it lifts up,
a suggestion, till

somewhere
the phone

rings, nurses
let it fall.

donia salem harhoor

thoth's bill

in egypt
baba speaks english
ibises
circle him
trilling   'arabi   'arabi
relax   your tired   tongue

Hannah Hirsh

CONFESSIONAL AS PRIMAL SCREAM

In New York everyone wears black
because we are in mourning for postmodernism.
Also we are very serious, our seriousness
is shown by our devotion to our markets and our margins.
Oh, the whirligigs of capitalism, they must keep turning,
they must keep churning out profit and purpose!
The city is perfect because people
are able to live alongside each other
like slightly anesthetized aliens
catching whiffs of each other's scents.
Imagine! As hominids traveling in nomadic tribes,
how often did we encounter strangers? It's a wonder
we don't kill each other more often on sight, with that
frantic dose of fear encoded in our hindbrains.
But here I go again, blaming evolution for all our failings.
I want to say it's unnatural, this intimacy—
my nose planted in a banker's armpit, his sweat
fertilizing my upper lip. So forget natural, America!
I'm putting my foot down on this fetish, our fixation
on "the raw stuff," our collective salivation
for the hi-fi cries of lions picking off the runts
of the zebra herd. Of course biology begets cruelty
when the only purpose of the gene is to propagate.
Yes, it's glorious to be an animal, but who
would want to be only animal?
None but Mr. Chairman himself,
our whiteface clown, ironclad ass in a lion's mask.
That I have never felt patriotic is perhaps
a failure of the imagination, but the phrase
"leader of the free world" has always struck me
as a kind of joke. Is there anything worse

than being ridiculed? I mean, besides being dead?
Men are afraid that women will laugh at them
and women are afraid that men will kill them
is a truism that regrettably bears repeating. We know
the fury of a woman scorned, but what of a man denied?
The postmodern world is ending. It matters to be alive.

AUBADE

if the oak leaves shimmer
lousy stars green with sun   if the cement

crack shudder open   if the earth
the water   if the moon waning

splashes into the alien depths of the pacific
if the waves raucous and folding like dough

if the dough kneaded by the knuckles of god
if the god is made flesh and the flesh saunters

slants toward sex   if the relics of joy
lie quiet beneath the morning mist

if I roll my body toward a warmth   if
that warmth be yours if you are already reaching

Nancy Kangas

THE END
Translated from the Spanish

I have left the human
that is as a brother to me.
Well, a brother about whom the clothes
do not stay sometimes.
All right. He is not a brother.
He is a person with whom every air
that comes in comes easy. (Not *every*,
please. Let's stay true. *Very much* of the air.)
He seems to make this air.

We built a house of ideas
as spectacular as the stars.

With together. For two years. Together
we were crazy with action. Together
we ran and ran towards the make,
everything all in the direction
to heaven. Voilà. Voilà voilà voilà.
During this time, I love the factories
that encircle his body. And he likes
that his hands are allowed on me.
All right.

And at the end of the run,
when up is the castle, he says,
Goodbye, sweet woman. I go now.
I say, *Goodbye, sweet man.*

And in the direction of small trees
I made a glass nothing of my stomach.
That is, I left everything in my stomach
on the earth.

If I was queen,
I would send this man that I love
with a love that feels that it started before
the life of me
whatever he likes.

(Sometimes now I send a photograph
of my small mountains, the girls from my body
to him and he says
aaah. And that is that.)
And oh, people. The day before today I said *I love you*
and it is new that he did not say *I love you, too.*
There are millions reasons
that he did not say this in this particular text
including the reason brutal.

Enough, please. Sleep, sleep, sad, sad queen,
who has the eyes of sad little dogs.
Let's look at the water that falls from the rocks.
Do you know what they do?
Fall. They fall and fall and fall.

It is possible that I will never
see him again, he who is my brother
but not a brother.
So, yes, go, waters of the eyes,
Go go go. If this is not the sad thing,
what is it?
Even all the small dogs are crying.

With the waters of the eyes falling
your face can be like a new penny.

Genevieve Kaplan

AT THE FOUNTAIN THERE IS MUSIC

Kindly get back.
Kindly would you please
acknowledge, maybe
ask about my own loss, look sideways or potentially
    deeply,
in those moments when all are both inside and outside
of themselves, the water moving yet determinedly
    contained.
Spraying and "dancing" and contained.
The reset button displays a recent conundrum: the sadness
of the world or the one universe
that recognizes loss differently: that sea, that cliff, that sea.
Embracing lions or forgetting them, embracing sea horses
    and sea dragons and sea stars.
Your lions are like dogs: they bark, they are sleek
wettened puppies, they don't yet know they live out of doors
because they've never yet been enclosed.

Once I was incredulous
about the possibility of stealing another's rhythm, because
    I'd heard, so clearly, the thievery.
I thought upon the spectrum of wrong-feeling things, those
    sounds were some
one shouldn't imitate, that one should only take apart
the thing that troubles, to begin with. Maybe I saw
some-thing—participated in some-thing—hung lagging on
    the cusp
of some-thing. Or perhaps by drawing attention I drew
a tension anew.

Ariana-Sophia Kartsonis

SQUAWBERRY MOON

A strawberry moon rose the last night
we packed our belongings away
as Jupiter hid from the mountainside
a strawberry moon-rose that night
that yellow-red fruit—huge spilled light
so that Jupiter drowned in the bay
of the strawberrymoonrosenight

Victoria Kornick

IVIg

Into various immaculate, or ivy-choked, gardens we walked together, community gardens or garden centers, or uncentered gardens, parks, the muddy shore of the river by our home, where one can stand with one foot in Maryland, one in Virginia, and another, if you are a dog, in the District of Columbia, the state lines etched on marble boundary markers, because here everything was political—

in vicious internal government squabbles, my father spent his early career, and stayed, even after he realized he would never work in politics.

I'm very incrementally grasping at the idea that, until four months ago, the initials IVIg meant nothing to me, not any of these possibilities, nor intravenous immunoglobulin, which sounds still to me like *into Venus I'm a goblin*,

like how, at a cocktail party, I met a woman whose husband's condition was much like my father's, and, who, when the doctor told her they would prescribe mycophenolate, heard Michael Finley, and eventually asked who Michael was and how he would be helping.

Dan is the name of the nurse who administers IVIg to my father in what had been my childhood bedroom, where my parents have thrown out the bed and moved in an office, though not taken down the 8th grade collage or the mesh screen of abandoned earrings, which hang above the whirring machine with its bright tubes attached to my father's arm.

My father cannot lift his hand to his ear, and when I call, I often forget I'm on speakerphone until my mother, or Dan, or someone walking past my father in a Target interjects their opinion:

driving a U-haul that far is gonna be a pain / have you tried acupressure for that? / congratulations!

It has been a year since my father got sick, and six months since he got a diagnosis, which on the WebMD page for uses of IVIg is not listed by name but as *other rare diseases*.

Necrotizing autoimmune myopathy is not common enough to have an acronym, but if it did I would say it like *name*, as in my father's name is not yet in remission, my father's name is responding to treatment, my father's name is Jim, short for James, the same name as my partner, so friends joke *how Freudian!* Michael Finley is administered orally for my father's name, as long as the patient can tolerate. My father's name means muscular death.

My father says *this is my favorite time of year* on any day that is beautiful, any season, all year. My father asks, when any new place is mentioned, if he can see it on a map. My father believes gardens are remarkable because, unlike houses or cars, they get better, not worse, over time.

Ted Lardner

SOMETIMES WHEN SOMETHING SADDENS ME I GROW MEAN

It's a miracle anything survives.
You can't steal something that's free.
The creek keeps splashing in my skull.
Some bones darken, some ache and turn to ash.

After a while my eyes stay open.
I begin to think I am riding
a bus, maybe, through the Holland Tunnel.
The waterfall turns to wheels.

Big tires whonk, two by two, the seams,
the same thoughts, over the lines.
What difference did having love ever make?
Who other than me is buried up here?

Seed by seed to the windward side of the mountain.
Seed by seed to the windmill side.
Seed of the seed of the mountain to the wind.
"*Say it*," say the Steller's jays.

My friend, who reaches in?
I can't explain the rocking.
The breeze has crept in my ribs and stayed.
I'd go anywhere to see her, any day.

Show me a bullet.
A portion of a flint-made blade.
Where were we going, when?
What were we going to do when we got there?

MY MOTHER IS LEARNING IN HER AUTHENTIC RELATIONSHIPS COURSE

Every union
must have a lover

and a beloved

as a hand
rubs the apple it's about to feed its own mouth, or

how a gemstone serves time
in the body of the watch, shining just as bright behind
    the silver back-plate

as it would on a finger.

Neither me or your father was either, she says

her eyes down in the red
stain at the bottom of her emptied glass

and I remember them together
at the kitchen table, going

over calendars. Gardening separate corners
of the yard, arguing over whose turn it was

to mow. Each kiss

on an expected date. Anniversary. New Years.
Anniversary. Acting out

the image of a marriage, neither one shining or thumbed.

This poem was published in *Tupelo Quarterly*.

Kateema Lee

WE CARRY

> after Nikki Giovanni's "Cotton Candy on a Rainy Day"
> & Lucille Clifton's "homage to my hips"

To be born a girl and brown is to be born between joy
and bruise. Some of us learn to carry calm and grief
in name-brand bags and in tight crossways of cornrow;
some walk around with a don't mess with me smile;

some carry the blues passed down from sinners
and saints, small breaches in rhythm wearing
away mask after mask, losing beats between hits.
Some of us sing between bills, between babies,

between absence and loss, between wigs, loosening
threads and burned ends, between lovers of big butts
and the ones who praise everyone's *round hips* but ours.
Sometimes we are like worn nonstick surfaces; we burn

anything that touches unprotected seams. Some of us learn
that love, at times, is a fist waiting to find a place to plant,
and living can be *cotton candy on a rainy day*. We learn
to savor and save the sweet, to make sugary, melting threads
respites of joy, to dance as what's left washes away.

Rob Lipton

GRACE

Imagine the conniptions Penelope throws when
her lawn, shitted up by her neighbor's Lab,
turns ocher brown, but okay, this is hardly
my fault, nor the scabbed half face of my
somewhere middle eastern gardener
Rami blowing leaves in a three piece suit
(not my sartorial vibe, but he handles the blower
like an NHL guard). We're talking god damn
forgiveness here! And I've heard John
Prine with his punch drunk voice
trundle through a gorgeous tune of
his forgiving just because it's finally
enough - to know he's been loved
no matter his fucking-up or lost his
throat to chew and infelicitous choices,
he's battered like a tin piñata, and features
his potato head visage equanimously
on his last CD.

This much is true – the poet has always
lost the fight, usually not even gone to war,
the kinetic battlefield is written out
in prose, and the poet is always in
a tactical retreat, watching intently
with range binoculars his own stunned
rise from trenches filled with boot camp
verbs rushing forward, head down, kitted out
with complete sentences up-armored against
metaphor.

From the infinite distance
of memory – measured in a Pico second after
you read this, measured in seasons
of the Jurassic, all the words of the universe
will claim their place, every poem that will
ever be written, even those where Elvis
never eats a fried banana and peanut butter
sandwich, where Mary Queen of Scott's
executioner is sobbing as the axe wavers
above her head - are printed out in the
foundational braille we use when holding
someone wounded by the suicidal charge
of those maimed, implacable nouns

Permeable membranes, we breathe this in
like diluted mustard gas, the lungs are
scared a little more each time, gentles
our resolve like our voices, like John Prine
forgiving the *syphilitic parasites*
biblically plaguing him
like the inevitably saintly Penelope
inviting her neighbor and the lab in for tea
the leaf-free lawn greening as it always will.

Masha Lisak

TO BRODSKY

You are always dying two months
after we walk the continent of cowboys,
though your northern Venice
was mine twenty-one years on.

In your other Venice I take a vaporetto
to the Quay of the Incurables,
which you sang in English,
which is erudite and smells of mothballs.

There is the splinter of your misogyny:
objects sublime and myopically faithful
described with a press of the lips,
and I let it stay though it suppurates.

On the subway, at night, I suck on the lollipop
of your poems, lowering the visard.

Emily Luan

池上

In 池上, the dogs sleep in the middle of the dark roads. They sleep with certainty, knowing that the cars and scooters of this town will trace a narrow path around them, preserving their dreams in the summer heat. I'd like to live with the kind of trust these dogs have, to lie down without fearing death. But when I bike by, my dessert dangling in my basket as the locals do, the dogs, they stand up and stare.

It's May, the swelling season, the rice fields a mirror of green. Even with the wind, stillness, a bicycle or tractor moving here and there, a figure in a white suit mixing pesticides in the back of his little blue truck. I'm not sure that anyone belongs here, the land cleared for miles but for the stray banyan trees along the empty road.

When it rains, snails.

如果狗也不認識我，那誰會呢？

On the train ride down the coast, I read a book beside a boy my age. I imagine that we're young lovers in a Taiwanese film, drawing open the curtain and looking out together when the ocean comes.

From the train, the ocean, and as we ride, the farther from it.

Christine H. Cummings

CONFESSION

When I was three, my first love was a weed growing under the drippy faucet in the back yard.

I remember we liked to laugh together, and how shiny her leaves were.

At nine the only one who understood me was the tall grass in the empty lot down the street.

I was so shy then it was a relief not to talk, and she was always rustling and whispering so I didn't have to.

In college I fell hard for Mary Jane but she got so fucking possessive and then she got crazy. I had to end that one.

Sometimes I still miss her.

Now I'm having a fling with Mugwort, or "Artemisia" as I like to call her.

We're just getting to know each other. So far it's going well, but you know, early days.

She's got a head (well, leaves and flowers and roots) full of dreams and she likes it when I wear lipstick and dresses.

Once in a while I give her a ride in my head so she can see through my eyes, walk around, stuff she can't do on her own.

She's down for it sometimes, prefers to stay home by the creek.

Laurie Macfee

CENTO OF BOOKS I'VE FOUND

                                                  and I can't see who's facedown
      a body floats in death
                                        in its window snow is always falling
I am not leaving the room
                                   shallow enough to cross, on the bank
           there is winter in her sleep
                                      or their eyes are "deceived"
           the buttons of a blouse; the bone was like pearl—
                             shoes I have never worn, I want to give them to a friend
     I paused long enough to encounter
                               oc•ci•put /óksiput/ n. back of the head
           my mother. But rather than be obvious
                                 some wrapped in rough cloth
I wonder how forgive could ever fit in my mouth
                                     in the way a famine is less—
     the ground was frozen, the coffin wood-burned
                            an indication of how long the pair have sung duets
mat•ter /máter/ n. 1 a physical substance
                                         head swinging toward the moon
   she starts to gather her things. I remain seated, the
                                           last rain, the first dazzle
         consumed, consuming : aria, easy
                  the tree which has pursued her since the storm bows its head to enter her dwelling
the secret illicit hairs
                                     my economy is a hand-me-down
        the bells inside me are quiet but
                                   one note emerges from the drizzle of sound
   to write I look for words in books

The structure is a cleave sonnet; regular text alphabetical down, superscript reversed alphabetical:

1. Ali, Kazim / Zamora, Javier
2. de la Torre, Mónica / Young, Dean
3. Hacker, Marilyn (translating Venue Khoury-Ghata)/Trethewey, Natasha
4. Hass, Bob / Shockley, Evie
5. Howe, Fanny / Rankine, Claudia
6. Kimiko Hahn / OED
7. May, Jamaal / Olds, Sharon
8. Olds, Sharon / May, Jamaal
9. Oxford English Dictionary / Kimiko Hahn
10. Rankine, Claudia / Howe, Fanny
11. Shockley, Evie / Hass, Bob
12. Tretheway, Nataaha / Hacker, Marilyn (t.Venus Khoury-Ghata)
13. Young, Dean / de la Torre, Mónica
14. Zamora, Javier / Ali, Kazim

Diane K. Martin

THE LAST TIME

He tried to teach me to waltz
on my wedding day, but the last
time he hit me I was sixteen.

Jeannette and Lauren were shouting
hurry! We needed to get out to the lake
before the sun warmed the ice.

He liked to make us stand at attention
for inspection. I hadn't made my bed
—so it was my fault he hit me.

He'd been a major in the war. I said
I would do it later. He hit me in the face.
When he came in for a second hit,

I caught his hand. His face turned red.
I thought this could be a heart attack.
I hoped his heart would explode. I

caught his hand, and I hit him back.
He used to say I would be first
woman president, then laugh. I cried.

I wouldn't let Jeannette and Lauren
hear me cry. The sun didn't warm the ice,
and I didn't make my bed, so I won, right?

He said I always lost the fight by being
emotional, just like a woman. He tried
to teach me to waltz on my wedding day.

I wouldn't waltz with him that day or ever.

Veronica Martin

GLOVING

What is there to say about a blue wall and a group of Acapulco
    daisies?

From this tempered blue, incessence seems as good an ending
    as ever.
Incessence, standing on the train with an arm over her head,
    one gloved
hand
holding on. The daisies going outside the warped window
    while the
handbag sways at eye-level. Years ago you told me the act that
    reads better
deserves to end the poem. So, say you can put smoke back into
    a cigarette.

So, the ghost of an image jumps any frame and arrives in the
    mind, replaying
over and again like a mantra or a working song or a chant.
    The artist stares

back at us through color. What mixing there. Going with the
    flow just far enough
to reach an end, whereupon the water keeps descending but at
    a greater force.
The daisies given away, the blue wall sinks back into itself.
    The glove falls
to the side of incessence and exits the car at an aboveground
    station, blotted by the sun.

Daria-Ann Martineau

SUDDEN AND NOT SO

Recall your friend, disappearing from this life

Sudden and not so—

strange headaches paralysis

diagnosed recovery relapse

hope
        that her extra years were worth it.

(You no longer close enough to ask her by the end.)

Who was she then, all her brain's remapping?

      not the same and so

was it so much *her* cancer who returned,

visitor you wouldn't recognize. She,

never again your Cherrie.

By the time news traveled to your phone—

Toronto Port-of-Spain New York

map by map satellite by satellite—

she had already left,

moving losing touch then

                        a final exit.
                        Why would anyone think to tell you
                        she was sick again?
To say goodbyes
                were, still, to be had?

This tumour, greedy for her company—

had it left some small lot in her mind
for you?

Nick Maurer

WESTERN MOTEL

On her way but to where? Room 206, spare, invaded by afternoon sun, the two-tone purple mountains, and the hood of the emerald car. This modern monument, rigidly mobile, hopelessly fast. I pour the drinks while she flattens roaches with the dark-brown book, still wearing the beige cloche to keep the falling plaster from her eyes as we lie down to think. The road has razored her stare to a sharp signal, she looks just past you, chewing up your own motionless planet. I want to be her, I want to be there, driving past the exits out of the slog of matter instead of syphoning the fumes of leveled turnoffs, this daily disappointing tinge. The sense I had of light as a constant then, on the wall beyond that wide solitary window, a limpid undisturbed medium yellow light, and what we put out there in the distance filled with even more light, a horizon ever-halving on route to the obsidian lake we drove to to swim and the dark slope she defined then ascended while I cut my teeth on a disappearing landmark.

Florencia Milito

TOTEM ANIMAL

The night before the parapolicías burned
my father's family house,
la casa de Ituzaingó,
taking particular care
to scorch a book about Cuba
on my very proper, Catholic grandmother's
nightstand, a gift
from her most irreverent son,
my mother had a prophetic dream
about an owl, its clipped wings, bulging
yellow eyes,
and knew we had to flee.
Se amamanta el terror,
passed down
in the mother's milk.
I carried with me
those eyes
into the dark blue
wreckage of exile,
their hypervigilance
now mine.

Kate O'Neill

INCOMING STORM

A real nor'easter teeming waters dangerous cargo

flood tossed skiffs   my boatman

my hanged man O scourge of rain   tempest   fury

my barn owl parapet   maritime warning   tidal squalls

my inlet prevailing gusts   albatross   hole in the hull

May Day May Day   surges   outages   widow's walk

jolt of lightning   crack   jetty   garnet dunes strewn

calamitous downpours   lack of foresight   toppled monuments

bruised cumulous   lighthouse blinking   breaking news

unsalvageable   devil's purse   barometric pressure   wave-tossed

shelter   in place   horseshoe crab shells   breakage

Pamela Paek

COLON: AERIAL VIEW
TWO PEOPLE, BACKS TURNED

Magnolia blossom
aggressed by ants

She mindkilled their fetus
into a reality of clotted blood

Light swallowed by shadow
burns a ring in each eye

If only marshmallow
peach blue flame
black crisps of ash
closedmouth joy

Yamini Pathak

DHARMA

A boy and girl ticketless on a clacking train
Not candy-cute even if you excavate
under the city dust that scabs their little
bodies from stringy hair to leathered soles

The children launch into the latest
Bollywood hit, tambourine thumping, all sex,
bump and grind in the sway and lurch of
commuters glued grim by sweat and purpose

They sing as if their lungs will burst
Tera husn hi jabardast dast
Tu cheez badi hai mast mast
You are the object of my lust, lust

Their voices rise over the furnace of wind and steel
as if they must shred the last fragment
of their skeletal chests
in an anthem to themselves

and their audience worn
by office files and cups of chai and cheap
smokes and the liquid heat before the monsoons
unzip the skies and before

the next stop the choristers unfurl
the flags of their palms, gather their lightweight
coins, at the door, squat and leap
into the flash and blur of the passing world

Sarah Peace

IF EVER

Is there a useful rumination
    A motherless question
    proceeds in the dark

It's possible   I am not for this world   and yet

    My prayers return unopened
    My eyes reflect repeated water

    If ever I arrive   in a moment of utter calm—

The day cracks and drips   unhinges light from meaning
A bird astounded by its own exuberance   recalls its loudest call

Emily Pérez

JEFFREY PINE

The naturalist asks us to smell it. Smell
is the gateway to memory.
I think that's what some book told me. I once loved
a Jeffrey, a boy, not a pine,
who grew to a painter, a man who died. Some people
smelled vanilla. I just smelled
the barkness. All smell dissolved when I birthed
my boys. Smell impeded
vomit free floors. Did Jeffrey smell of vanilla?
I don't think he used Drakkar Noir,
the scent of our south Texas youth. Probably Polo
by Ralph Lauren, which marked
his sophistication. Lauren was really Lifshitz.
I think that's what some book
told me. A creature seeking camouflage.
Jeffrey loved the Moonlight Sonata,
and for him I learned to play it. Though I never
played it for him. It was my next
to last grand gesture. A mating call for a man. The last
when I shaved my legs.
That was in my political days. A creature
seeking camouflage. I don't
know much about nature. At least, I don't
remember. All memory dissolved
when I birthed my first boy. Memory impeded
more birthing. On an evergreen island
with the help of a book, I couldn't tell
pines from firs. Their pinecones
and their needles. I remember
genus pinus. I never
told Jeffrey I loved him.

Then he dated my best friend. Of course
he pressed her for sex. We didn't think
it was rapey. Remember, this was the 80s.
A teen girl's ideal was a stalker who stood
on the hood of his car. Just outside
her window. Nothing impeded
mating. I never saw Jeffrey's casket.
Though we were both at the lake,
and we each took a turn, he never
saw me on water skis. Even after
he cajoled me. I was a preteen
with a wedgie. Jeffrey died
of a growth in his brain. I never
saw his paintings.

Michael A. Reyes

TODDLER

You may or may not know that toddler derives from toddle,
    which means to wobble.
You may or may not know that a toddler is one to three
    years old. In this poem,
I want to speak about the three-year-old toddler. The toddler's
    attention is short

and change of toys occurs at frequent intervals. The toddler
    of whom I speak of likes to kick
pebbles into the gutter, or at least try to. The toddler of
    whom I speak of also likes to bend
for dandelions, sometimes plucking them. It's common for
    the toddler to play in stable

squatting positions, their feet set wide and bottom not quite
    brushing the ground.
They might need to hold on to a thing to stand up again. At
    three, the toddler begins to see
themself as a separate individual. However, they still see
    other toddlers as objects.

The toddler may kick another toddler as if a pebble into the
    gutter or the toddler may bend
to tap the toes of another toddler. Self-awareness arrives to
    the toddler sometimes
after 18 months of age, though later in age isn't uncommon.
    At three, the toddler most likely

recognizes themself as a separate physical being with their
    own thoughts and actions.
Along with self-recognition come feelings of
    embarrassment and pride

that the toddler hadn't previously experienced. You may or
    may not have noticed

that I haven't mentioned anything about the parent. In this
    poem, memory is the only parent
the three-year-old toddler will have. In this poem, I did
    research first before beginning
and still feel as if I'm dancing around the image of which
    this poem first leaped from.

I didn't intend for this poem to be an elongated definition
    on toddler.
I began this way to arrive to my sister.
She was three years old when she stood in front of a judge,
    barely peering over the table.

She was asked to plead her case for not being removed from
    the US,
to prove she was not "dismissible." She was labeled
    "unaccompanied"
although her mother arrived at the border with her for asylum.

Her mother was deported days before this removal proceeding.
My sister could not sit still and slipped off the courtroom
    chair. She attempted to climb
the table and when she wasn't allowed to, she wobbled her
    way under it.

My sister calls this her first moment of resistance and
    invites me to smile with her,

though she never makes much eye contact nor speaks much
    about the new mother
that adopted her after the judge ordered her into foster care.

This ending makes me think of all the pebbles I've kicked
    today,
how they arrived at my feet and how they will arrive at
    someone else's.

This poem was published in *Queen Mob's Teahouse* special issue "Where Are the Children?"

Corinna Rosendahl

NO HUNGRY

                Too hot

Gently
pinch the food in like salt

It hurts to crack

    my clothes off

Even that

    When you shatter

    someone

they are the smallest bones
of your hands

and you want to vomit

Both of us
    begging

across ruby-colored carpet
and I can't pick us up—

I am thrown into the burning blossoms

I am torn out

Flames down my thigh

I put my bright body in the bath
Smash cold water on my face
to get the burning off

You appear

because I don't think you can

you are leaning against the door frame

Wind splashes
through the window

Do you feel that
You whisper

                     to no one

My pulse blinking
into your body

Absolutely

    Anything

to make you alive for me again

Kalen Rowe

MY BIG STUPID BIGOT STATE

Most of it's empty.
Good.

Still,
there are enough

idiots to fill
an emptiness

with what idiots
call speaking

their mind.
Great, tremendous

idiots ruled here.
Even God

wanted Greg Abbott
dead.

God felled
a tree on him

during his morning
jog.

Instead,
Greg donned

a wheelchair,
thus becoming

the worst human
in a wheelchair.

With one wrinkly
white hand

a bigot holds a bible,
with the other,

a red hot hand,
smelt of evaporated blood,

permanently fisted,
he razes sanctuaries

and feeds
on the graves

of fetuses
through knuckles.

What idiots.
What stupid

fucking idiots.
What stupid,

stupid bigots.

Perry: bigot.

Bush: idiot.
Bush 2: big idiot.

One time,
in Houston,

a bunch of
birdbrained

beefy bigots
calling themselves

white lives
matter

(really
calling into question

if they do)
they drove

all the way
from the Woodlands

(redneck affluents)
to "protest"

a closed NAACP
building.

Of course,
they got their own

precinct.
Of course,

some wore
red laces

and carried
rifles.

Of course.
The state

finds space
to store

its bigots
(in its heart)

its wrested
children

(cages
in the desert)

its lost
immigrants

(garbage
bags stuffed

in shallow
mass graves).

There are many
good things, too,

but you have to
look small and be big.

You have to
make it

through all
the hating

emptiness.
There is love

here, too,
it's true:

everything's
bigger in Texas.

Brett Shaw

WHEN YOU ARE AWAY ALL MY MEMORIES ARE TACTILE

    1

                            2

       3

4

           5

                     6

                7

---

[1] You're leaving / early & out of sync with our usual clock / the loafing / the love in bed / slow-building friction of spoons / metal to metal / & soon / static / shocks to touch

[2] Your words soft blooming mariposas / their supine geometries / delicate / self-sufficient / I remember mostly your tracing me / neck-back to shoulder blade / soft bite on the cheek of my ass / an exclamation

[3] Up without you / the world oscillates / concentricities of maintenance / & space / everything radiates / resonates / toasted cumin / garlic / sautéed mushrooms / the eroticism of a bowl of eggs broke with cream / the shuffle of pencil my two feet

[4] Afternoons & the mind wanders to you / imperceptibly & then steady falling the sound like rain / I walk to bed / undress & find the underwear you left for the pug / you / you / you against my face / I descend

[5]Wondering what it is for you / to be entered / I pull my underwear half-down / the way you like when you want me fast / balls pressed against stalk / tendril / creeping vine / cotton smooth against your thighs / close / you slide a finger through the unripe plum of my ass / quick pit / we want / our fingers there / at the root of the body what is unfathomable

[6]You call / catching me near my own end / tangled in bedsheets / ask me to wait / & I hear through the phone the precise way you step when you walk with intention / at your office door the sound of the steel lock bolting through wood nearly undoes me

[7]You start gently / one finger against yourself / as when we've only watched / pensive in a way that makes my own ministrations boorish / your other hand at my base / we desire / the tango of contradiction & release / & I know in the end you'll have your three fingers triangled reaching for a center swung distant then closer / one hand against your left breast / lode star / & I am milk against myself / oil derrick for your breaths which grow calmer now / though still clasping that rush of flight there / our silence across the phone soluble / as satisfied tongues are stable / at rest

Michael Sinck

[IF YOU READ THIS   BEAR DON'T BE SCARED   WE'RE BACK WALKING THE DEERPATH BEHIND YOUR DAD'S HOUSE]

if you read this   bear don't be scared: we're back walking
    the deerpath behind your dad's house
reedgrass golden up to your earlobes   our summer stretch
    i count the hoofprints and forget

open heat in the easement   transmission towers holding
    heavy miles of high tension line
animals bed down in the latticework their shadows make:
    we lay in last season's white fur

the empty pellet guns   our empty shirts like blankets under
    us: the day is late   but growing longer

Kathleen L. Taylor

SELVING

All the parts are Me—creaturegodmachine.

Mimetic of someones to homecome for:
zoomorphic shadowplague complexes,
occupiers of this willed skull parlor.

I, beings stumped on the human structure,
(how to hook them up to refuse-tissue)
conceive coventry covens subconscious.

I tests communion of head and body,
ratcheting manifest feeling-figures.

If I un-figures them, they continue
themselves cellular for my appendage—
appendix, or other contact comforts.

Thinking my Me a mess from pedigree,
I open my rooms to strangerous species.

Jay Aquinas Thompson

THEY HAVE TAKEN ME FROM THE WORLD

But I am not of this world.

Wouldn't you be tempted, too, to start the poem
with a spin of gossamer that then stiffens subtly till it shatters,
mild numinous detail of stirring fir
and puzzled ghost and, reader slowly realizes, the *after* of grief
and only then the dying father—*smash*—

But does the body have something to teach about what the spirit is for?

but I share first instead the shards so you know what my father was before he was a ghost:

the baby he'd grown late in Stage Four to be, systems one by one running into stillness, fluids that settled as their laborious equilibrating ran down, belly swollen, nerve still singing somewhere in there to nerve, ice chips and Naked Juice and tea-colored urine, curled arms that rose blind above blankets, heels propped against soring. The church of it was impossible: his breath a deep laborious snore, snore like a birth-cry, cartoon lungs lifting more than they could bear, nothing in the room singing nor knowing its appointed hour, the changing air eager to be caught in him for his last breath, every apple-pip of lymph and intestinal flora floating right on that eager edge of timelessness,

But what was your father before he was a ghost?

and now my father's ghost—slipping briefly swallow-light
from the impersonal collective all-sustaining
labor of the dead—comes curious back to
the world of becoming he's no longer of.

But remember his breath was a deep laborious snore.

The ghost bends astounded over a cup of coffee as it cools;

(do you need me to remind you what time is, Dad?
now that the world runs astoundingly on though
you've stepped away?)

over ponderosas trampled
beneath the hooves of a century's stags;

over a head of coarse hair growing till it's matted
suddenly with blood;

over a night shell
washed up worn smooth: I feel your stare!

But his rapt doubt is really yours.

Ghost, this is becoming: someone votes; someone lives
    another night
on syrup sandwiches; someone swipes cans, juice, diapers,
    chicken
across a bleeping barcode buddy for their eight hours;

someone sharpies a sign to carry
outside the clinic federal dollars (more blood, paper blood)
    aim to starve.

Ghost, this is time: listen tonight with me to the crackle of
    wax getting
eaten by fire, to a kid holding her breath
then letting it explosively out.

Time is a leaf skeleton, a bootprint filling, a hunger strike
    laying a
pattern of repeated refusal forward, and you're in
none of it, none of it. Watch.

But on the night of this drive your father wasn't even a
    ghost yet.

The DJ turns the gentle pulse of his techno down
long enough to say *rain soon* and sure enough,
on the windshield of this silent car,
silent streets, the first drops.

I pull up outside your house, Dad
(this is two weeks before, Finn asleep inside too),
step out to rain on me warm and sporadic,
mildness, mildness,
gravel crunch-crunching,
mildness, mildness, mildness,
firs tossing slow and benign
against the city-orange midnight sky!

Eden Werring

THE TWO EDENS

Imagine there are two Edens here—one supernal,
    one wreckage.
See how they sit together, quiescent and looming on
    a rattan bench.
Their hands, baskets to hold the other.
Their hearts, wet brooches pinned to their dresses.
An incarnadined thread snakes the space between
    their heads.
They tell parables for foxes and parables for lentils.

The first Eden is a vanishing garden, the maiden
    without eyes.
The first wanders paths of unerasable orchards lit by
    lambent fruit.
The first Eden makes the granola from scratch.

The second Eden sees through narcissus eyes, herself
    in the rearview mirror.
The second's mind is a weak soup.
The second cremates herself daily, swallows her own slag,
    chokes bone.

The first Eden's head skylights to cerulean light, a chorus
    of eucalyptus.
The first performs arias composed by nightblooming
    jasmine, by cardamom.
The first Eden is negative-capable.

The second Eden scrapes the seeds from her husband with
    the back of a knife.
The second got caught stealing resume paper from the
    campus bookstore senior year.

The second Eden smears herself into the cracks of her
	mistakes.

The first Eden has alchemical hair, each strand a witchy,
	blue filament.
The first bakes crostatas ombred by stone fruits she just
	picked from warm French trees.
The first Eden has three hearts, like an octopus.

The second Eden neglects that platonic zucchini in the
	fridge until it melts to yellow.
The second's veins writhe, splashing menstrual syrup.
The second Eden forgets the first Eden.

Everyone must have two pockets, goes an old Hasidic
	saying, to use as we will.
Submerge your hand in the first pocket and retrieve a
	string of seven words:
For your sake was the world created. The message in
	the other pocket:
I am dust and ashes.

Maybe there really aren't two Edens sitting here, but one.
I'm talking to you, Garden.

Emily Wolahan

ALL TALES ENORMOUSLY UNKNOT MEMORY

I cannot say before or

when or after.

I was in a place—not here, not remotely

near here. I like camels. They were the first animals

I saw tame, their enormous bodies kneeling down,

limbering, maternal. I see women who walk

exactly like my mother when she still walked

and observed. Lately she's a Diebenkorn,

the way he paints women with no faces,

turned away but looking, thought implied but not evident,

little shared. She's *Woman on a Porch*,

sitting with her arms on the arms of the chair,

face in fleshy shadow, bands of color behind her,

band of water, sand bar, bare sky.

She's not facing the view (inscrutable).

My mother in the morning, her iPad propped up,

reviewing headlines, arms on the table either side of
   the device

like lines in a parking lot stretching towards the car as it
   pulls in.

I cannot say   before   or

when   or   after.

View of Notre Dâme—the spare blue one from 1914

that Matisse painted in the spring. He made the outline,

sketched in details, then washed it all blue, a watery blue,

undulating colors, a bridge, the blue Seine—

apart from a green hedge and the hedge's shadow,

apart from the shadow of the towers, the cathedral
   followed around

by blackness. Everything pared down to its most simple
   gesture,

inscrutable and recognized,

the spatial depth of under a bridge formed

by the suggestion of an arc. The white corner of the nave

a portal just above the center of the painting

drawing us into the spring of 1914—the spring.

There's the before.

Here's the when: speaking to her when she's

chopping or stirring or drinking her wine,

is speaking to the white portal of before.

The speaking folds in, but it's never coming out. Lately

I see things because of the ring of light emitted
   around them,

the dust mark left by a vase removed. Lately, it's a collision

of lines, a bit of color, of canvases made, some time ago,

available only on loan.   Formless, faceless—these belie
   the feeling.

Marcene Gandolfo

BEES IN WINTER

I believe the violin's quivered ring
waves through

the gristly palm of this geography.
The piano's

unhinged keys play a perfect octave.
I believe feral

ghosts of devotion find sweetness
inside a frozen hive.

Jack Martin

CROSSING THE RIVER

I admit it. I don't know.
I don't know who the god of sleep is.
Google says, In Greek mythology

the personification of sleep was Hypnos.
Is it still Hypnos? Or is it our Commander and Chief?
Netflix? Google? I don't remember my password.

I admit it. Some of the things I'm about to tell you:
lies. Why not? Others, pure truth. All of the rest,
frivolous conjecture. But the absence of knowing

is not sleep. If there were a password for sleep,
would you use it. Happiness? Unhappiness?
Some things can't be fixed.

And who would want to anyway?
Others things can't be forgiven.
Like mosquitoes. Those little bastards.

If it weren't for the sting
and the itch,
I could bear them.

In another context, the whine of their wings might be
    adorable,
that high-pitched trill, teeny-tiny bird song, shrunken
    trumpet.
What else is there to do about mosquitoes?

Stay inside?
Make clothes out of the same thing we make screen doors?
What is the difference between raw meat and my body?

Meat doesn't sunburn. Meat doesn't care when you cook it.
Meat doesn't try to understand grace or beauty or loss.
Mosquitoes won't eat raw meat.

What is the difference between beauty and loss?
Both are in the soil beneath us. Can loss be beautiful?
Do you remember my wife?

Grace is a different story. Grace is love for the unlovely;
peace for the restless; mosquito netting to the delicious.
The only other option is to forget. Or to sleep.

While I am asleep, someone fills my bedroom
with oranges, the little ones, clementines.
Well, maybe it's not fair to say "fills,"

but there are many. Almost waist deep,
up to the level of the mattress where I'm sleeping.
I awake. The room smells like breakfast.

I sit up in bed, hang my feet over, wiggle
them down past the oranges, down until
my toes reach the floor. I wiggle them down

until I am flat-footed. I stand and try sliding
feet slowly, one at a time, like moving through
mud or deep snow, toward the door.

The door is closed. I stop a few feet away.
I grab clementines by the handful
and throw them on to the bed.

The doorway is not clear, but I turn the knob
and pull. The door opens a little at a time smashing
rinds of many oranges. Juice runs between my toes.

I would enter the hallway, but it is waist deep in pears.

Bob Hass

CONFESSIONAL POETRY

Bless me, Father, for I have sinned.
It has been two weeks since my last confession
And these are my sins—
Except at age seven in the spring
As you were preparing for First Communion
At which you would receive the body
And blood of Jesus in the form
Of a small white wafer while you were dressed
In a white shirt, white pants and even
a pair of white leather shoes
Which, if you were a boy, you would
Never wear again. First Confession
Was so that you would be radiantly
Prepared to receive God into your body
And in that case you could say
This is my First Confession (it did
cross my mind that this was something
The priest already knew, but formulas
Can be deeply comforting until they aren't.)
The hard part, Sister Rosemary conceded,
Was thinking up the sins to say.
Not obeying your parents was a dependable one.
Also swearing. Also being glad if bad things
Happened to people you didn't like.
I don't remember what I contrived
To say on the first occasion. You entered
What was called 'the confession box,'
A sort of closet where the priest sat
Behind a screen and you knelt to speak
To him and he listened and then
Told you to say one Our Father
And three Hail Mary's, and to make

A good act of contrition, and you said
The words the sisters had helped you
To memorize and then you would go
To the main altar and kneel and say
The prayers which were called 'your penance.'
The act of contrition went like this:

O my God, I am heartily sorry
for having offended Thee,
and I detest all my sins,
because I dread the loss of heaven
and the pains of hell. But most of all
because I have offended Thee, my God,
who art all good and deserving
of all my love. I firmly resolve
with the help of Thy grace,
to confess my sins, to do penance
and to amend my life. Amen.

After you said it the priest would mutter
Something in Latin and make a sign
of the cross in the air you could dimly see
That totally erased your sins from the heavenly record,
Only it didn't happen in heaven, the nuns
Had emphasized, it happened inside you.
One day, walking home from school,
After the Friday confessions, my friend
Janet Caetano confided to me a discovery
She had made. She had confessed
to Father O'Meara, the pastor of our parish,
St.Raphael's, named for the angel who came
to earth and healed people with his hands,

That she had peed outdoors in the open fields
Where we played hide and seek and conducted
Wars by hurling lengths of wild fennel
At one other and he had told her
That peeing outdoors wasn't a sin
Which I was very glad to hear, but I also
Wondered if the obscure feeling that hearing
this information from Janet had produced
in me might be a sin. I knew I could ask
a priest—I thought I might pick one
of the younger ones—but I couldn't quite
figure out how to frame the question.

Evie Shockley

in) visibility

my first time on the mountain, i learned
    there was a puppy-sized hole in the atmosphere
around brett's heels. that absence lucille called
    milo, dedicating one of her week's drafts
to his memory. without her poem, i might have missed
    how he was missed. being new, i saw
not milo's shade, but his little white shadow,
    shadowing brett. lucille read her poem
on thursday night.   what can memory do
    with things it barely or never had? i carry with me
some foggy notion about eyes of two different colors
    or a single floppy ear: milo, whom i did not know, distinct
in the penumbra of lucille's regard.

time lurches on. now, milo's shadow, toby, has cast
    a shadow of his own. i have never seen brett without
a cloud of energy swirling around her feet,
    and felix must seem as inevitable to this year's
newcomers as toby did to me, back when lucille's
    moon was full. but i see, orbiting the office behind
them, the toby-sized hole: rounder, closer
    to the ground. i fill it with my memory of his quick
tongue and trot: brett's darling with the cheerfully
    protective bark, her white knight.

—*for bhj*

Charles Halsted

THE YEAR THE SOX WON THE PENNANT

I was an eight-year-old kid at the end of the War
when Pete, a fly-boy in the Army Air corps,
was liberated from a Nazi camp for POWs,
came home to marry Ellie, our upstairs boarder.

Pete had grown up in a western Mass town.
A minor league player before the War,
he taught me to hit, run, and catch, took me
to Fenway in Boston to watch his beloved Red Sox.

It was the same ballpark where Babe Ruth
first played, before the remote owners traded
him off to the hated Yankees of New York,
throwing the Sox into decades of doldrums.
(It did not take me long to learn Red Sox lore.)

But then came the day when a new player
was paid to erase all memories of the Babe.
His name was Ted Williams, he grew up in CA,
and his batting averaged .406 in '41.

Though away in the Navy in World War II,
fighting for our country, just like Pete,
Ted came back full force in '46, when
he batted .342, led the legendary Sox
to their first American League pennant
in eighteen years.

It was during that year that Pete and I sat
in Fenway's left-field stands, looking down at
Ted when the other team was at bat.
When the Sox were up, he often got hits, the longest
ever home run in June of that year, confirming
his hero status in my then nine-year-old brain.

When our Sox faced the St. Louis Cardinals
in the World Series, my fourth-grade
classmates and I were glued to a squawk box
with a scratchy-voiced announcer when each
school recess rolled around. After game six,
Ted was injured and out, and the Series was tied.

It was back to St. Louis, October fifteenth, game
scores even with two out in the eighth, Cardinals
at bat, when a country boy named Enos Slaughter
made an eighth-inning dash from first base to home
plate, to win the game, take the World Series,
a calamitous day in Red Sox lore. They would
not win it all for fifty-eight years more.

Tamam Kahn

THE WELL AND BABA FARID

chillah-i ma'kus (a rope is tied round the feet of the one
suspended upside down in a well for forty days and nights.)

He came to Delhi to un-make himself,
just hanging by a thread, feet to the sky,

the pressure in his eyeballs unbearable. Death
is said to occur in 8 to 10 hours. Cartilage stretched.

Did his hip joints pop? Hours of pain. Baba Farid
hung in search of perfect love. He was just

a boy and his teacher sent him there to do this.
Blood pounded, sped up. Alone in the well. The muezzin

Lowered him after the call to prayer, deep in the night,
then pulled him up at dawn, without anyone else knowing.

So slowly or all-at-once he twisted, shivered and shone.
Then he spoke: *I love none in the two worlds but you, God.*

Each of the 40 nights his ankles were tied, the rope heavy
inside the circle of stones damp and dark, as his eyes closed.

Did he sink into sadness? Kiss the threshold with sweetness
as he was lowered into his rough round house of love?

Baba Farid, 13th century Sufi mystic and poet, is recognized today in India and Pakistan Punjabi communities by scholars, Sufis and Sikhs and many others.

Mónica de la Torre

DIVAGAR

> "There's a lot of waiting in the drama of experience."
> —Lyn Hejinian, *Oxota*

No signal from the interface except for a frozen half-bitten
    fruit.
Other than that, no logos. An hour is spent explaining

to the group what I've forgotten, to do with the
    mistranslation
of a verb that means *drifting* but can imply deviance.

The next hour goes by trying to remember, in the back
    of my mind,
the name of the artist who makes paintings on inkjets.

Why I'd think of him escapes me. Now my gaze circles
    the yoga bun
of the tall woman in front of me. I didn't pay $20 to
    contemplate

the back of her head. It's killing me. The pillars and plaster
saints with their tonsures floating amid electronic sound
    waves.

At such volume they could crumble. The virgin safe in a
    dimly lit
niche as the tapping on my skull and the clamor of bones
    or killer

bees assaults the repurposed church. This is what I sought,
    while

in another recess I keep hearing Violeta's *"Volver a los
    diecisiete"*

and seventeen-year-olds marching against the nonsense
    of arming
schoolteachers. If I were an instrument. A bassoon. In the
    source language

we don't say "spread the word." *Corre la voz* is our idiom,
    easily
mistaken for a voice that runs. From the back row all I see
    is fingers

gliding in sync with her vocalizations. How fitting her
    last name
be Halo. Lucky for us here time is measure and inexplicable

substance. That's when I decide to stop fighting the city.
    Use it in my
favor. Speak to strangers. Demolish the work in the
    performance.

Jesse Nathan

POEM

Birds singing in the morning to say
They survived the night,
To talk vigorously with other birds
About how they were not eaten in the night
By owl, were not
Taken in the day by kite.

The Poets

Kazim Ali was born in the United Kingdom to Muslim parents of Indian, Iranian, and Egyptian descent. He received a BA and MA from the University of Albany-SUNY, and an MFA from New York University. His books comprise several volumes of poetry, including *Sky Ward*, winner of the Ohioana Book Award in Poetry; *The Far Mosque*, winner of Alice James Books' New England/New York Award; *The Fortieth Day*; *All One's Blue*; and the cross-genre text *Bright Felon*. His novels include the recently published *The Secret Room: A String Quartet* and among his books of essays is *Fasting for Ramadan: Notes from a Spiritual Practice*. Ali is an associate professor of creative writing and comparative literature at Oberlin College. His new book of poems, *Inquisition,* and a new hybrid memoir, *Silver Road: Essays, Maps & Calligraphies,* were both released in 2018.

Mónica de la Torre is the author of six books of poetry, most recently *The Happy End/All Welcome* (Ugly Duckling Presse). Born and raised in Mexico City, she translates poetry, writes about art, and is a contributing editor to *BOMB* Magazine. Publications include *Triple Canopy, Harper's, Poetry, The White Review, Erizo, the New Yorker*, and *huun: arte/pensamiento desde México*. She teaches in the Literary Arts program at Brown University.

Robert Hass is a poet, translator, and essayist. Ecco/HarperCollins recently published his most recent books of essays, *A Little Book on Form: An Exploration Into the Formal Imagination of Poetry* and *What Light Can Do: Essays 1985-2010*. His other recent books include his selected poems, *The Apple Trees at Olema* (Ecco/HarperCollins), *Time and Materials* (Ecco/HarperCollins), which was awarded the Pulitzer Prize and the National Book Award, and his edition of Walt Whitman's *Song of Myself and Other Poems* (Counterpoint). His other books of poetry include *Sun Under Wood: New Poems, Human Wishes, Praise,* and *Field Guide*. He has also co-translated many volumes of the poetry of Czeslaw Milosz and is the author or editor of several other collections of essays and translations, including *The Essential Haiku: Versions of Basho, Buson, and Issa; Twentieth Century Pleasures: Prose on Poetry;* and *Now & Then: The Poet's Choice Columns 1996-2000*. He served as Poet Laureate of the United States from 1995 to 1997.

Awarded a MacArthur Fellowship and the National Book Critics Circle Award twice, he is a professor of English at UC Berkeley and directs the Poetry Program of the Community of Writers at Squaw Valley. http://www.barclayagency.com/site/speaker/robert-hass

Sharon Olds is the author of eleven books of poetry. *Stag's Leap*, published by Knopf in the US and Jonathan Cape in the UK, was awarded the 2012 T.S. Eliot Prize and the 2013 Pulitzer Prize. *The Dead and the Living* received the National Book Critics Circle Award. *The Unswept Room* was a finalist for the National Book Award and the National Book Critics Circle Award, and *One Secret Thing* was a finalist for the Forward Prize and the T.S. Eliot Prize. Olds teaches at New York University's Graduate Program in Creative Writing and helped to found the NYU workshop program, now in its thirtieth year, for residents of Goldwater Hospital on Roosevelt Island and for veterans of Iraq and Afghanistan wars. In 2015 Olds was elected to the American Academy of Arts and Letters. In 2016 The Academy of American Poets awarded Olds the Wallace Stevens Award. Sharon Olds's most recent collection, *Odes,* was published by Knopf in 2016. www.sharonolds.net

Evie Shockley is from Nashville, Tennessee. Recent collections of poems include *semiautomatic* (2017), a finalist for the 2018 Pulitzer Prize, and *the new black* (2011), winner of the 2012 Hurston/Wright Legacy Award in Poetry, both published in the Wesleyan Poetry Series. Evie Shockley has also published the critical study, *Renegade Poetics: Black Aesthetics and Formal Innovation in African American Poetry* (2011). Her poems and essays appear widely in journals and anthologies. Evie Shockley's honors include the 2015 Stephen Henderson Award for Outstanding Achievement in Poetry and the 2012 Holmes National Poetry Prize. Currently serving as creative editor for *Feminist Studies,* Shockley is Associate Professor of English at Rutgers University–New Brunswick.

Jabari Jawan Allen is a Chicago, Illinois native. A 2018 Tin House Winter Workshop Scholar and 2018 Lucille Clifton Memorial

Scholar, Allen has received support from Community of Writers at Squaw Valley, Kenyon Review Writers Workshop, and VONA/Voices. Allen's poems have appeared or are forthcoming in *Virginia Quarterly Review, Vinyl, Four Chambers,* and elsewhere. He currently lives in Phoenix, Arizona.

Dan Alter can be found working on poems in San Francisco trains and Berkeley cafes, driving too fast, holding a meal in one hand and talking on the phone, washing dishes dishes dishes his family leaves in their merry wake, or online at danalter.net. He makes a living getting covered with icky stuff on construction sites.

Ethan Andrews lives in Portland, Maine and works as a baker. He is grateful to his girlfriend, Liz, for introducing him to poetry and for being his first and most generous reader. Besides writing and mixing cookie dough, Ethan enjoys playing golf and courting his two aloof cats.

Joan Baranow directs the MA Humanities and the Low-Residency MFA in Creative Writing programs at Dominican University of California. Her poems have appeared in *The Gettysburg Review, The Paris Review, Spillway, Poetry East, JAMA, Feminist Studies,* and other journals. With her husband, David Watts, she produced the PBS documentary *Healing Words: Poetry & Medicine.* Her second film, *The Time We Have,* is a feature-length documentary about poetry writing and palliative care.

Sherah Bloor is a South African doctoral student at Harvard University, where she studies continental philosophy, medieval mysticism, and poetry.

Jay Brecker lives and work in southern California. His poems have appeared in *New Mexico Review, RHINO, OVS Magazine, Bird's Thumb, Squaw Valley Review, [dialog box],* a chapbook from Thistle and Weed Press, and www.onehundredwalkers.com. His manuscript, *A Case of Mad Love,* was semifinalist in the 2015 Trio House Press open reading.

Jeremy Cantor began writing after a career in laboratory chemistry. Six poems from his debut collection, *Wisteria from Seed* (Kelsay Books, 2015), arranged for mezzo-soprano and accompaniment by Dr. Robert Gross, have been performed at the Boston Conservatory. Jeremy's poems have appeared in *ISLE* (Interdisciplinary Studies in Literature and the Environment) and other journals.

Elizabeth Biller Chapman has been a member of the Squaw Valley Community of Writers since 2000. Her poems have appeared in *Poetry, Santa Clara Review, Water-Stone Review, Poet Lore, Blueline,* and *Rattle. Creekwalker,* a chapbook, was published by (M)other Tongue Press (1995), and her collection *Candlefish* was published by the University of Arkansas Press (2004). The collection *Light Thickens* (Ashland Poetry Press, 2009) was awarded the Robert McGovern Prize.

James Ciano earned an MFA in poetry from New York University, where he was a Goldwater Hospital fellow. His recent work can be found in *jubilat* and *Prairie Schooner* and has been supported by New York University and Vermont Studio Center. A native of Syosset, New York, he currently lives and works in Los Angeles, California.

Jolie Elizabeth Clark lives in Oakland, California with her daughter. Her poems have appeared in the *New England Review, Hayden's Ferry Review* and other publications. Attending the Community of Writers at Squaw Valley is her favorite thing to do.

Judy Brackett Crowe lives in the Sierra Nevada foothills in California and has taught English composition, literature, and creative writing at Sierra College. Her poems have appeared in *Epoch, The Maine Review, Catamaran, burntdistrict, Commonweal, Cultural Weekly, The Midwest Quarterly, West Marin Review, Miramar, Subtropics, Crab Orchard Review, and elsewhere.* Her chapbook, *Flat Water: Nebraska Poems,* will be published by Finishing Line Press in 2019.

Christine Holland Cummings lives in Menlo Park, California with her husband, a retired physicist, and dog, a change of career service dog puppy. In 2019, she too was set free from her corporate marketing job and now spends great chunks of time doing better things like gardening, learning herbalism and practicing other witchy arts. Her poems have appeared in *Writer's Resist, Dark Matter: Women Witnessing, Reckoning, Bellowing Ark, Blueline, Hamilton Stone Review, Blue Arc,* an anthology of California poets from Tebot Bach Press, and a poetry anthology about loss of companion animals titled *Our Last Walk.* Christine has an MFA from the Bennington College Writing Seminars.

Armen Davoudian's poems and translations from Persian have appeared or are forthcoming in *The Sewanee Review, Waxwing, The Yale Review* and elsewhere. His work has been awarded scholarships from Bread Loaf, the Sewanee Writers' Conference, and the

Community of Writers at Squaw Valley, and residencies from the Millay Colony and Lighthouse Works. He grew up in Isfahan, Iran and is currently pursuing a PhD in English at Stanford University.

Rosa De Anda has worked as a member of the International Longshoremen and Warehousemen's Union, in the Californian fields, and as community arts administrator, teacher, and interpreter. She considers the words *tolerance, the other, minority, and people of color* inappropriate and substandard to describe the world's talented and brilliant populations. "As linguistic architects, we can use our art to establish sustainable relationships and document the human experience."

Michael Anna de Armas is an MFA student at Warren Wilson College and has studied the craft of poetry at the Palm Beach Poetry Festival and the Bread Loaf Orion Environmental Writers Conference. She resides in Coconut Grove, Florida, with her husband, two lively daughters, and many wild peacocks.

Julie Sevilla Drake, after making most of her life in Alaska, now writes from Fidalgo Island, Washington. In addition to being a poet, Drake is an artist and quiltmaker, whose abstract art has been exhibited all over the world.

Danny Duffy has worked as a proofreader, an editorial assistant, and a writer-in-residence at an art museum. Currently, he is an MFA candidate in The Writing Seminars at Johns Hopkins University. He has received scholarships from the Community of Writers at Squaw Valley and the North Street Collective. His poems appear in *The Times Literary Supplement* and *Poet Lore.*

Jay A. Fernandez is a writer, editor, and arts journalist whose work has appeared in *The Washington Post, the Los Angeles Times, The Hollywood Reporter, Time Out New York, Boston Review, USA Today, Los Angeles, Premiere, Columbia Journalism Review,* and other publications. A 2017 fiction fellow at the Community of Writers, he is currently a fiction editor at Los Angeles Review of Books focusing on literary criticism and essays. A Philadelphia native, he lives with his wife and sons in South Pasadena.

Marcene Gandolfo has taught writing and literature at several northern California colleges and universities, and she currently teaches writing for Women's Wisdom Art, a nonprofit organization that provides art instruction to women in the Sacramento community. Her debut book, *Angles of Departure,* won *Foreword Review*'s

Silver Award for Poetry in 2015. Her poems have been published widely in literary journals, including *Poet Lore, Bellingham Review, and December Magazine.*

Kelsey Gutierrez is an MFA candidate at California State University, Long Beach, where she teaches poetry and composition and serves as poetry editor of the program's journal, *RipRap*. The recipient of the 2016 William T. Shadden Memorial Award, Kelsey was also selected as one of *Literary Women*'s Harriet Williams Emerging Writers for 2019. Her work has appeared in *Coe Review, Muse,* and *Broad! Magazine.*

Jessica Guzman is a doctoral student at the University of Southern Mississippi. Her work appears or is forthcoming in *Pleiades, Ecotone, Shenandoah, Tin House*'s Broadside Thirty Series, and elsewhere. Jessica reads for *Memorious*.

Charles Halsted is a retired academic physician at the University of California, Davis. His poems have appeared in *Blood and Bourbon, Blood and Thunder, Chest, Clerestory, Contemporary Poetry, Degenerates, Edify Fiction, The Gambler, The Ghazal Page, Haibun Today,* and many other journals. He has attended Stanford Continuing Studies, the Summer Fishtrap Writers' Conference, the Community of Writers at Squaw Valley, and the Taos Writers Conference. His first chapbook was published in November 2018 and a full book is in press.

donia salem harhoor is an Egyptian-American co-conspirator with her 11-year-old cub. She is Executive Director of The Outlet Dance Project, a principal dancer and choreographer with Sakshi Productions, and part of the Brown Girl in the Ring Collective. She has an MFA in Interdisciplinary Art from Goddard College. In 2016, harhoor was artist-in-residence with Swim Pony, and she is an alumna of Urban Bush Women's Summer Leadership Institute. Her poetry has appeared in *Anomaly, Ballet Review,* and *Sukoon* magazines.

Hannah Hirsh earned her BA in Classics from Princeton University (2016) and is currently pursuing her MFA in poetry at NYU (2019). She is from central New Jersey and lives in Brooklyn.

Brionne Janae was the recipient of the 2016 St. Botoloph Emerging Artist award. She is a Hedgebrook and Vermont Studio Center alumna and proud Cave Canem Fellow. Her work has appeared at the *Academy of American Poets,* and in *American Poetry Review,*

Sun Magazine, Los Angeles Review, Rattle, Bitch Magazine, Cincinnati Review, jubilat, Sixth Finch, Plume, Bayou Magazine, The Nashville Review, Waxwing, and *Redivider* among others. Brionne's first collection, *After Jubilee,* was published by Boaat Press. www.brionnejanae.com

Tamam Kahn has presented her poetry at conferences including The Sidi Chicker World Meeting of Tassawuf Affiliates in Marrakech, Morocco. She is the author of *Untold: A History of the Wives of Prophet Muhammad* (International Book Award 2011) and *Fatima's Touch: Poems and Stories of the Prophet's Daughter* (International Book Award Finalist 2016). She was awarded a writing residency at Jentel Foundation and has attended Ragdale Foundation twice.

Nancy Kangas launched *Nancy's Magazine* in the early 1980s in San Francisco, a collection of comics, literature, and advice. Today she writes humor for *Muse* (a magazine for young readers), and leads workshops around Ohio and beyond. Her poems have appeared in numerous books and journals and have been nominated for a Pushcart Prize. The poetry column, "Slides (Interpreted by Nancy)," regularly appears in the online journal, *Ohio Edit*. Kangas is co-director and producer of "Preschool Poets: An Animated Film Series."

Genevieve Kaplan is the author of *In the ice house* (Red Hen Press), winner of the A Room of Her Own Foundation's poetry publication prize. She has also published three chapbooks: *In an aviary* (Grey Book Press), *travelogue* (Dancing Girl Press), and *settings for these scenes* (Convulsive Editions). Her poems have recently appeared in *Spillway, Third Coast, The Laurel Review,* and *Copper Nickel*. She lives in southern California, where she edits the Toad Press International chapbook series of contemporary translations.

Ariana-Sophia Kartsonis, author of *Intaglio,* Kent State University Press, 2006, and *The Rub,* Elixir Press, 2015, teaches at Columbus College of Art & Design. She serves as the faculty advisor for *Botticelli Literary/Art* magazine.

Victoria Kornick holds an MFA from New York University, where she was a Rona Jaffe and Goldwater Hospital fellow. She has received support from the Elizabeth George Foundation and the Saltonstall Foundation for the Arts, and her work appears in *At Length Magazine, Nashville Review,* and *The Greensboro Review,* among other publications. She is currently a PhD candidate in Creative Nonfiction at the University of Southern California.

Ted Lardner teaches at Cleveland State University. His work has appeared in or is forthcoming from *Blue Fifth Review, Arsenic Lobster, DIAGRAM, Bird's Thumb,* and other journals. His chapbook, *We Practice For It,* selected by Mark Doty for the Sunken Garden Poetry Award, was published by Tupelo Press in 2014.

Jessica Lee grew up in Nevada City, California, and currently resides in the Pacific Northwest. She is an Assistant Poetry Editor for *Narrative Magazine* and an Editorial Reader for Copper Canyon Press. Her work has appeared or is forthcoming in *BOAAT, cream city review, Diagram, Fugue, Passages North, Phoebe, Prairie Schooner, Zone 3,* and elsewhere. Find her online at readjessicalee.com.

Kateema Lee is a Cave Canem graduate fellow, a Callaloo fellow, and a participant of The Home School. Her recent work has appeared in *Baltimore Review, Beltway Poetry Quarterly, African American Review, Gargoyle,* and other journals. A Washington, D.C. native, Kateema is the author of the chapbooks, *Almost Invisible* and *Musings of a Netflix Binge Viewer.*

Rob Lipton is the current poet laureate of Richmond, California. He has been a Pushcart nominee and Gregory O'Donoghue Competition winner. His work has appeared in *Interbang, Jacaranda Review, King Log, Shades of Contradiction, The Texas Observer, Parthenon West, New Orleans Quarterly, Journal of Human Architecture, Quillpuddle, Opium Magazine, Red Wheelbarrow,* and *Southword.* His book, *A Complex Bravery* was published by Marick Press. See the photo Rob's poem references at: pitchfork.com/reviews/albums/john-prine-tree-of-forgiveness/

Masha Lisak lives in Oakland, CA, where she works as a consultant for social sector organizations and occasionally walks dogs. Her poetry is forthcoming in *Sycamore Review.*

Emily Luan has been awarded fellowships from the Community of Writers at Squaw Valley, Art Farm, and the Fine Arts Work Center, and is currently an MFA candidate in Poetry at Rutgers University-Newark. Her poetry has appeared or is forthcoming in *Grist, Epiphany,* and elsewhere. A Taiwanese-American poet from northern Massachusetts, Emily earned a BA in English and Creative Writing from Middlebury College.

Laurie Macfee, an artist, and nonprofit arts administrator in addition to being a poet, has coordinated and directed the writing program at Vermont Studio Center and coordinates lectures for the UC Berkeley

Center for New Media and the Arts Research Center. Her poems have appeared in *Forklift, Ohio, Ninth Letter, Tupelo Quarterly, Jet Fuel Review*, and the anthology, *Change in the American West*. She has shown her visual art nationally and abroad.

Diane K. Martin lives in western Sonoma County, California. Her work has appeared in *American Poetry Review, Field, Kenyon Review, Harvard Review, Zyzzyva, Plume*, and *Best New Poets*, among others. Diane's poems have received a Pushcart Special Mention, and won a poetry prize from *Smartish Pace*. Her collection, *Conjugated Visits*, a National Poetry Series finalist, was published in 2010 by Dream Horse Press. Her second book, *Hue and Cry*, will be published in 2019 by MadHat Press.

Jack Martin is a high school teacher in Colorado. His poems have appeared in *Ploughshares, Georgia Review*, and other journals.

Veronica Martin is a writer from Portland, Oregon. Her poems and essays have appeared in *Vestoj, Kinfolk, Tin House*'s "The Open Bar," and other publications. She holds an MFA from University of Texas at Austin.

Daria-Ann Martineau was born and raised in Trinidad and Tobago. Her poems have appeared in *Anomaly, Narrative*, and *The Collagist*, among other journals. A Pushcart-nominated poet with an MFA in Poetry from New York University, Daria-Ann is an alumna of several writing conferences, including Bread Loaf and Idyllwild Arts Writers Week.

Nick Maurer holds an MFA from the University of California, Irvine. He lives in California.

Florencia Milito was born in Argentina, spent her early childhood in Venezuela, and has lived in the US since she was nine. A bilingual poet, essayist, and translator, she's an alumna of Hedgebrook, CantoMundo, and the San Francisco Grotto, and her work has appeared in *Zyzzyva, Indiana Review, Catamaran, Entremares, Diálogo, the anthology Latina Voices, Protest*, and *Struggle in 21st Century USA*, and other journals and anthologies.

Jesse Nathan studies literature at Stanford and lives in San Francisco. His recent work has appeared in *Boston Review, The Nation, American Poetry Review*, and elsewhere.

Kate O'Neill holds an MFA from IAIA, and an EdD from Harvard University. Her poetry appears in the *Taos Journal of the Arts*, the *Journal of War, Literature and the Arts*, *Pangolin*, and *Poetry Ireland Review*, among others. She was a Vermont Studio Center resident in 2018 and teaches at University of New Mexico, Taos.

Pamela Paek spends most of her time, when not on the road for work, exploring the world and reminding people she doesn't like to be called Pam or filming her cockatoo Chilly and his many crazy antics. She writes poetry infrequently, but when she does, it's with high intensity over long blocks of time. She never knows what to include in bios and fears that what was excluded could have been more interesting.

Yamini Pathak was born in India and lives in New Jersey. Her writing has appeared or is forthcoming in the *Kenyon Review, Rattle, Journal of New Jersey Poets*, and the *Hindu*. Yamini is an alumnus of VONA/Voices (Voices of Our Nations Arts Foundation). She says that she is at her most creative when designing Halloween costumes for her kids.

Sarah Peace is a recent graduate of the MFA Programs in Writing at the University of California, Irvine, where she is currently a lecturer in the composition program.

Emily Pérez is the author of *House of Sugar, House of Stone* and the chapbooks *Backyard Migration Route* and *Made and Unmade*. A CantoMundo fellow, her poems have appeared or are forthcoming in journals including *Copper Nickel, Poetry, Diode*, and *The Fairy Tale Review*. She teaches English and Gender Studies in Denver, where she lives with her husband and sons.

Michael A. Reyes is a graduate student in English at Cal State Los Angeles and writes for *Spider* children's magazine. He has received fellowships and recognition from VONA/Voices, Home School, PEN America Los Angeles, Anaphora Writing Residency at Otis College of Art and Design, and the Community of Writers at Squaw Valley.

Corinna Rosendahl lives in Portland, Oregon. Her work has appeared in *Gulf Coast, Salt Hill, Verse Daily, Hayden's Ferry Review, The Carolina Quarterly, Linebreak*, and elsewhere. She earned her MFA in poetry at the University of California, Irvine.

Kalen Rowe has a degree in creative writing from the University of Houston. His poetry has appeared in *No Assholes, The Letters Page, Gravel,* and elsewhere. In 2013, he helped found and now runs Anklebiters Publishing, an underground bookmaking studio that publishes and helps self-publish journals, books, and zines in Houston, Texas.

Brett Shaw was born in Los Angeles. He sang opera and was an oil and gas accountant. His work is forthcoming in *BOAAT Journal* and *Reservoir*. He holds an MFA from the University of Alabama.

Jacqueline Hughes Simon is a poet living in Berkeley. Her poems have appeared in *The Cortland Review, Poecology,* and *Squaw Valley Review*.

Michael Sinck lives and writes in Riverside, California.

Catherine Staples is the author of *The Rattling Window* and *Never a Note Forfeit*. Her poems have appeared or are forthcoming in *Gettysburg Review, The Kenyon Review, Poetry, The Southern Review, The Yale Review, Commonweal, Terrain,* and elsewhere. Honors include a McGovern Prize, a Dakin fellowship from Sewanee Writer's Conference, the New England Poetry Club's Daniel Varoujan and Barbara Bradley Awards, and a Tyrone Guthrie residency at Annamaghkerrig. She teaches in the Honors and English programs at Villanova University.

Kathleen L. Taylor studied narrative medicine and poetry in the Creative Writing and Writing for Performing Arts MFA at the University of California, Riverside, where she served as poetry editor for *Santa Ana River Review*. Her work has appeared in *Foothill Journal, New Limestone Review, Peacock Journal, Southern Women's Review, The McNeese Review, Turtle Island Quarterly,* and *White Stag Journal*. Her poem, "Bonding with Bad Mother," was nominated for a Pushcart Prize by *New Limestone Review*.

Jay Aquinas Thompson is a poet, teacher, essayist, parent, spouse, and spiritual creature. He has recent work in *COAST | No COAST, The Spectacle, Denver Quarterly, Fog Machine, Big Big Wednesday* and *Poetry Northwest* where he's a contributing editor. He lives in Seattle with his family, where he teaches poetry to public school students and incarcerated women.

Eden Werring lives in Redding, Connecticut with her husband and two children. She received a BA in English Literature from Yale University and is currently pursuing an MFA at Sarah Lawrence College. Her poems have appeared in the *Yale Literary Magazine* and an interview with Sarah Manguso appeared in *LUMINA*. Werring was a graduate student reader at the Sarah Lawrence Poetry Festival. Her book-in-progress about guilt, *Work On What Has Been Spoiled,* was shortlisted for the 2018 Graywolf Press Nonfiction Prize.

Emily Wolahan is the author of the poetry collection *Hinge*. Her poems have appeared in *Oversound, The Georgia Review, Boston Review,* and *Gulf Coast,* among other places. She is senior editor at Two Lines Press and an affiliate artist at the Headlands Center for the Arts.

Colophon

Written Here: The Community of Writers Poetry Review 2018 was set using the slab serif Archer (a font, in the words of the designers, that hits "just the right notes of forthrightness, credibility, and charm") for the poems, and Chalet Comprimé ("compact yet uncompromising") for the names of authors and other headings.

Happenstance Type-O-Rama
www.happenstance.net

Proceeds from the sales of
Written Here: The Community of Writers Poetry Review 2018
benefit the Community of Writers Poetry Scholarship Fund

www.ingramcontent.com/pod-product-compliance
Lightning Source LLC
Chambersburg PA
CBHW032128090426
42743CB00007B/516